MANGA SHAKESPEARE®

OTHELLO

ADAPTED BY

RICHARD APPIGNANESI

ILLUSTRATED BY

RYUTA OSADA

Published by
SelfMadeHero
139-141 Pancras Road
London NW1 1UN
www.selfmadehero.com

This edition published 2017

Illustrator: Ryuta Osada
Text Adaptor: Richard Appignanesi
Designer: Andy Huckle
Textual Consultant: Nick de Somogyi
Publishing Director: Emma Hayley

ISBN: 978-0-9558169-5-6

10 9 8 7 6 5
Printed and bound in Slovenia

"O my fair warrior!"

Othello, the valiant Moor of Venice, has married
Desdemona – without her father Brabantio's consent.

"When I love thee not,
chaos is come again!"

"Heaven keep
that monster
from Othello's mind!"

Iago, a junior officer in Othello's staff

"I hate the Moor!"

Lieutenant Michael Cassio,
Othello's newly promoted deputy

"I have lost my
reputation!"

Brabantio, father to Desdemona

"She has deceived her father — and may thee!"

"I will drown myself!"

Roderigo, hopeless suitor to Desdemona

The Duke of Venice and his Senators

"Othello, we must employ you against the enemy…"

"I'll after that villain!"

Montano, Governor of Cyprus

Emilia, wife to Iago, companion to Desdemona

"What will you give me for that handkerchief?"

Bianca, a good-time girl, friend to Cassio

"What did you mean by that handkerchief?"

Gratiano, a nobleman of Venice
"Poor Desdemona!"
Lodovico, a messenger from Venice
"This would not be believed!"

Our story begins in Venice, during the Carnival season...

VENICE AT NIGHT.
IAGO EXPLAINS TO RODERIGO HIS
GRIEVANCE AGAINST OTHELLO...

THREE GREAT ONES OF THE CITY SUIT TO MAKE ME HIS LIEUTENANT. I AM WORTH NO WORSE A PLACE.

BUT SAYS HE, "I HAVE ALREADY CHOSEN MY OFFICER."

AND WHAT WAS HE?! ONE MICHAEL CASSIO, A FLORENTINE, THAT NEVER SET A SQUADRON IN THE FIELD!

BUT HE, SIR, HAD THE ELECTION, AND MUST HIS LIEUTENANT BE...

GULP!

NOW, SIR, BE JUDGE YOURSELF, WHETHER I IN ANY JUST TERM AM AFFINED TO LOVE THE MOOR.

I WOULD NOT FOLLOW HIM THEN.

IN FOLLOWING HIM, I FOLLOW BUT MYSELF — FOR MY PECULIAR END.

YOUR FAIR DAUGHTER CLASPS A LASCIVIOUS MOOR.

SATISFY YOURSELF IF SHE BE IN HER CHAMBER.

CALL UP ALL MY PEOPLE!

THIS ACCIDENT IS NOT UNLIKE MY DREAM!

LIGHT, I SAY! LIGHT!

FAREWELL, FOR I MUST LEAVE YOU.

IT SEEMS NOT WHOLESOME TO MY PLACE TO BE PRODUCED AGAINST THE MOOR.

THOUGH I DO HATE HIM, YET I MUST SHOW A SIGN OF LOVE.

YOU SHALL LEAD THE SEARCH, AND THERE WILL I BE WITH HIM.

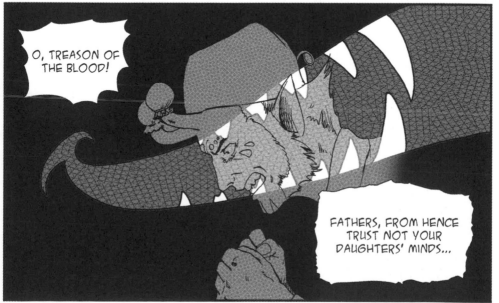

RODERIGO, DO YOU KNOW WHERE WE MAY APPREHEND HER AND THE MOOR?

I THINK I CAN DISCOVER HIM, IF YOU PLEASE GO ALONG WITH ME.

PRAY YOU, LEAD ON.

GET WEAPONS, HO!

ARE YOU FAST MARRIED?

BE ASSURED OF THIS: BRABANTIO WILL DIVORCE YOU, OR PUT UPON YOU WHAT RESTRAINT THE LAW WILL GIVE HIM.

LET HIM DO HIS SPITE.

MY SERVICES SHALL OUT-TONGUE HIS COMPLAINTS.

IN THE COUNCIL CHAMBER, WORRYING NEWS HAS REACHED THE DUKE OF VENICE AND HIS SENATORS.

THESE NEWS DO ALL CONFIRM A TURKISH FLEET BEARING UP TO CYPRUS.

HERE COMES BRABANTIO AND THE VALIANT MOOR.

WHOEVER HE BE THAT BEGUILED YOUR DAUGHTER, THE BLOODY BOOK OF LAW SHALL READ.

HERE IS THE MAN, THIS MOOR!

WHAT CAN YOU SAY TO THIS?

IT IS TRUE, I HAVE MARRIED HER...

LITTLE OF THIS GREAT WORLD CAN I SPEAK, MORE THAN PERTAINS TO FEATS OF BATTLE...

AND THEREFORE LITTLE SHALL I GRACE MY CAUSE IN SPEAKING FOR MYSELF.

OTHELLO, SPEAK.

DID YOU POISON THIS YOUNG MAID'S AFFECTIONS?

SAY IT, OTHELLO.

HER FATHER OFT QUESTIONED ME THE STORY OF MY LIFE, THE BATTLES, SIEGES, FORTUNES THAT I HAVE PASSED...

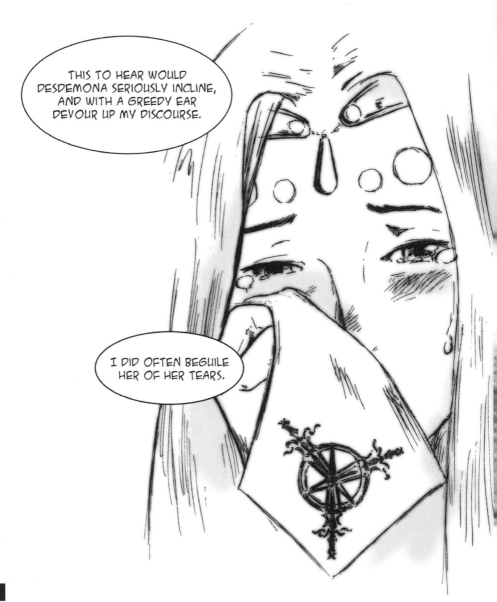

COME HITHER, GENTLE MISTRESS.

DO YOU PERCEIVE IN ALL THIS NOBLE COMPANY WHERE MOST YOU OWE OBEDIENCE?

I DO PERCEIVE HERE A DIVIDED DUTY.

I AM HITHERTO YOUR DAUGHTER; BUT HERE'S MY HUSBAND.

AND SO MUCH DUTY I PROFESS DUE TO THE MOOR MY LORD.

CUSTOM HATH MADE THE STEEL COUCH OF WAR MY BED OF DOWN.

I DO UNDERTAKE THESE PRESENT WARS AGAINST THE OTTOMITES.

I CRAVE FIT DISPOSITION FOR MY WIFE.

IF YOU PLEASE, BE IT AT HER FATHER'S.

I'LL NOT HAVE IT SO.

NOR I.

NOR WOULD I THERE RESIDE TO PUT MY FATHER IN IMPATIENT THOUGHTS BY BEING IN HIS EYE.

WHAT WOULD YOU, DESDEMONA?

IF VIRTUE NO DELIGHTED BEAUTY LACK, YOUR SON-IN-LAW IS FAR MORE FAIR THAN BLACK.

LOOK TO HER, MOOR, IF THOU HAST EYES TO SEE...

SHE HAS DECEIVED HER FATHER, AND MAY THEE.

HONEST IAGO, MY DESDEMONA MUST I LEAVE TO THEE. LET THY WIFE ATTEND ON HER.

COME, DESDEMONA, I HAVE BUT AN HOUR OF LOVE TO SPEND WITH THEE.

THEREFORE PUT MONEY IN THY PURSE.

THOU SHALT ENJOY HER.

WILT THOU BE FAST TO MY HOPES?

THOU ART SURE OF ME. I TELL THEE AGAIN, I HATE THE MOOR.

IF THOU CANST CUCKOLD HIM, THOU DOST THYSELF A PLEASURE, ME A SPORT.

GO, PROVIDE THY MONEY.

THE VENETIAN FLEET BEGINS TO ARRIVE IN CYPRUS, MET BY MONTANO, THE GOVERNOR OF THE FORT.

MICHAEL CASSIO, LIEUTENANT TO THE MOOR OTHELLO, IS COME ON SHORE.

PRAY HEAVEN FOR BRAVE OTHELLO!

LET THE HEAVENS GIVE HIM DEFENCE AGAINST THE ELEMENTS, FOR I HAVE LOST HIM ON A DANGEROUS SEA.

WHO HAS PUT IN?

'TIS ONE IAGO.

TEMPESTS THEMSELVES, HAVING SENSE OF BEAUTY, LET GO SAFELY BY THE DIVINE DESDEMONA.

WHAT IS SHE?

OUR GREAT CAPTAIN'S CAPTAIN, LEFT IN THE CONDUCT OF THE BOLD IAGO.

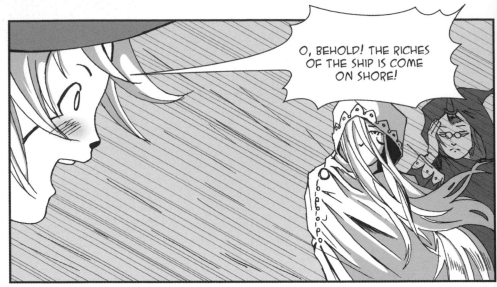

O, BEHOLD! THE RICHES OF THE SHIP IS COME ON SHORE!

I THANK YOU, VALIANT CASSIO. WHAT TIDINGS CAN YOU TELL ME OF MY LORD?

HE'S WELL AND WILL BE SHORTLY HERE.

WELCOME, MISTRESS.

GOOD IAGO, 'TIS MY BREEDING THAT GIVES ME THIS BOLD SHOW OF COURTESY.

SIR, WOULD SHE GIVE YOU SO MUCH OF HER LIPS AS OF HER TONGUE SHE BESTOWS ON ME, YOU'D HAVE ENOUGH.

WHAT WOULDST THOU WRITE OF ME, IF THOU SHOULDST PRAISE ME?

YOU SHALL NOT WRITE MY PRAISE.

O GENTLE LADY, DO NOT PUT ME TO IT, FOR I AM NOTHING IF NOT CRITICAL.

Nothing shall content my soul till I am evened with him, wife for wife, or put the Moor into a jealousy so strong that judgement cannot cure. I'll make the Moor thank me, love me, and reward me for making him egregiously an ass!

'TIS HERE, BUT YET CONFUSED.

KNAVERY'S PLAIN FACE IS NEVER SEEN TILL USED.

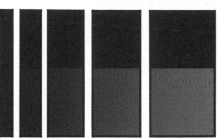

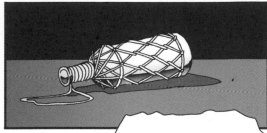

DO NOT THINK, GENTLEMEN, I AM DRUNK... THIS IS MY RIGHT HAND, AND THIS IS MY LEFT HAND. I CAN STAND WELL ENOUGH AND SPEAK WELL ENOUGH...

NOW, AMONGST THIS FLOCK OF DRUNKARDS AM I TO PUT OUR CASSIO IN SOME ACTION THAT MAY OFFEND THE ISLE.

BUT HERE THEY COME.

EXCELLENT WELL.

YOU SEE THIS FELLOW? I FEAR THE TRUST OTHELLO PUTS HIM IN.

HIS INFIRMITY WILL SHAKE THIS ISLAND.

BUT IS HE OFTEN THUS?

'TIS EVERMORE THE PROLOGUE TO HIS SLEEP.

IT WERE WELL THE GENERAL WERE PUT IN MIND OF IT.

HIS GOOD NATURE PRIZES THE VIRTUE THAT APPEARS IN CASSIO, AND LOOKS NOT ON HIS EVILS.

IT WERE AN HONEST ACTION TO SAY SO TO THE MOOR.

NOT I, FOR I DO LOVE CASSIO WELL —

BUT HARK! WHAT NOISE?!

YOU ROGUE! YOU RASCAL!

I AM HURT...
LIEUTENANT, HOLD! YOU WILL BE SHAMED FOR EVER!
ARE WE TURNED TURKS AND DO THAT WHICH HEAVEN HATH FORBID THE OTTOMITES?!
HONEST IAGO, SPEAK. WHO BEGAN THIS?

I DO NOT KNOW. I CANNOT SPEAK ANY BEGINNING TO THIS PEEVISH ODDS.

HOW COMES IT, MICHAEL?

PARDON ME, I CANNOT SPEAK.

WORTHY MONTANO, WHAT'S THE MATTER THAT YOU UNLACE YOUR REPUTATION THUS FOR THE NAME OF A NIGHT-BRAWLER?

CASSIO, I LOVE THEE, BUT NEVER MORE BE OFFICER OF MINE.

LOOK IF MY LOVE BE NOT RAISED!

WHAT'S THE MATTER?

ALL'S WELL NOW, SWEETING. COME, DESDEMONA, 'TIS THE SOLDIER'S LIFE TO HAVE THEIR SLUMBERS WAKED WITH STRIFE.

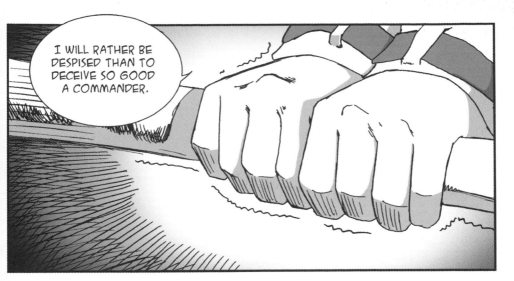

I WILL RATHER BE DESPISED THAN TO DECEIVE SO GOOD A COMMANDER.

O THOU INVISIBLE SPIRIT OF WINE! LET US CALL THEE DEVIL!

I — DRUNK?!

YOU OR ANY MAN LIVING MAY BE DRUNK AT SOME TIME.

IN THE MORNING I WILL BESEECH THE VIRTUOUS DESDEMONA TO UNDERTAKE FOR ME.

I AM DESPERATE OF MY FORTUNES.

GOOD NIGHT, HONEST IAGO!

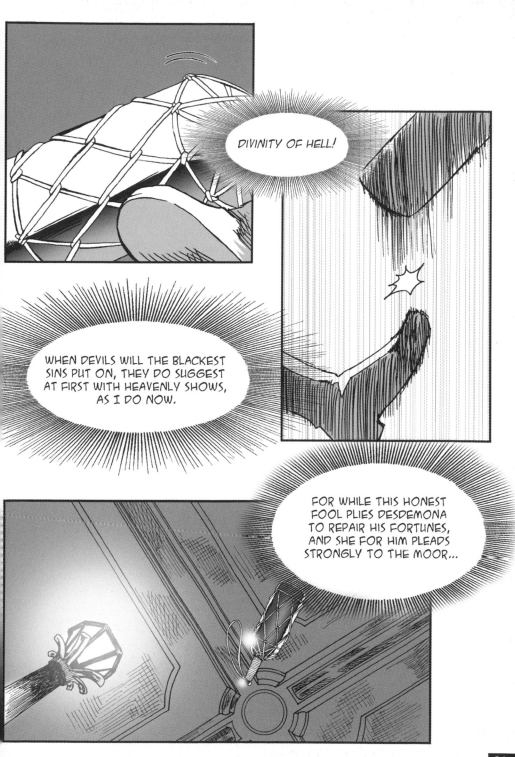

RODERIGO!

MY MONEY IS ALMOST SPENT.

I HAVE BEEN TONIGHT EXCEEDINGLY WELL CUDGELLED — AND SO, WITH NO MONEY AT ALL, RETURN AGAIN TO VENICE.

HOW POOR ARE THEY THAT HAVE NOT PATIENCE!

I BESEECH YOU, GIVE ME ADVANTAGE OF SOME BRIEF DISCOURSE WITH DESDEMONA ALONE.

PRAY YOU, COME IN.

I KNOW IT GRIEVES MY HUSBAND, AS IF THE CASE WERE HIS.

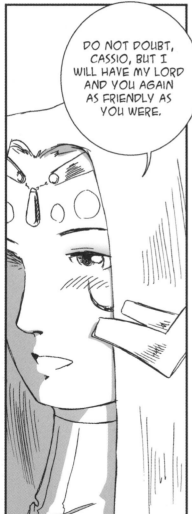

DO NOT DOUBT, CASSIO, BUT I WILL HAVE MY LORD AND YOU AGAIN AS FRIENDLY AS YOU WERE.

MADAM, WHATEVER SHALL BECOME OF MICHAEL CASSIO, HE'S NEVER ANYTHING BUT YOUR TRUE SERVANT.

I KNOW YOU DO LOVE MY LORD.

HA! I LIKE NOT THAT.

WAS NOT THAT CASSIO PARTED FROM MY WIFE?

CASSIO, MY LORD? NO, I CANNOT THINK THAT HE WOULD STEAL AWAY SO GUILTY-LIKE, SEEING YOU COMING.

I DO BELIEVE 'TWAS HE.

I SUFFER WITH HIM. GOOD LOVE, CALL HIM BACK.

NOT NOW, SWEET DESDEMONA, SOME OTHER TIME.

BUT SHALL IT BE SHORTLY? NAME THE TIME, BUT LET IT NOT EXCEED THREE DAYS.

LET HIM COME WHEN HE WILL. I WILL DENY THEE NOTHING.

O YES, AND WENT BETWEEN US VERY OFTEN.

INDEED?

"INDEED"? AY, INDEED. DISCERN'ST THOU AUGHT IN THAT? IS HE NOT HONEST?

"HONEST", MY LORD?

I KNOW THOU ART FULL OF LOVE AND HONESTY, AND WEIGH'ST THY WORDS BEFORE THOU GIV'ST THEM BREATH...

THEREFORE THESE STOPS OF THINE FRIGHT ME THE MORE.

CASSIO, I DARE PRESUME, IS HONEST.

NOR WILL I DRAW THE SMALLEST FEAR OR DOUBT OF HER. FOR SHE HAD EYES, AND CHOSE ME.

NO, IAGO, I'LL SEE BEFORE I DOUBT — WHEN I DOUBT, PROVE.

THERE IS NO MORE BUT THIS: AWAY AT ONCE WITH LOVE OR JEALOUSY!

I HUMBLY DO BESEECH YOUR PARDON FOR TOO MUCH LOVING YOU.

I AM BOUND TO THEE FOR EVER.

I SEE THIS HATH A LITTLE DASHED YOUR SPIRITS.

NOT A JOT, *NOT A JOT.*

I ONCE MORE TAKE MY LEAVE.

THIS FELLOW'S OF EXCEEDING HONESTY AND KNOWS ALL QUALITIES OF HUMAN DEALINGS.

O CURSE OF MARRIAGE — THAT WE CAN CALL THESE DELICATE CREATURES OURS, AND NOT THEIR APPETITES!

I had rather be a toad, and live upon the vapour of a dungeon, than keep a corner in the thing I love for others' uses.

Desdemona comes.

If she be false – o, then heaven mocks itself!

I'll not believe it.

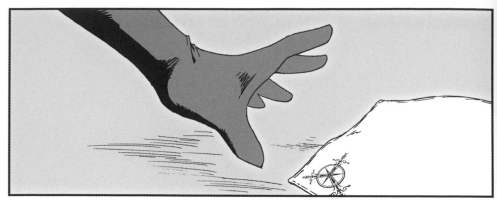

I AM GLAD I HAVE FOUND THIS NAPKIN.

THIS WAS HER FIRST REMEMBRANCE FROM THE MOOR.

MY HUSBAND HATH A HUNDRED TIMES WOO'D ME TO STEAL IT — BUT SHE RESERVES IT EVERMORE ABOUT HER TO KISS AND TALK TO.

I'LL GIVE IT TO IAGO.

WHAT HE WILL DO WITH IT HEAVEN KNOWS, NOT I.

I NOTHING KNOW BUT TO PLEASE HIS FANTASY.

WHAT DO YOU HERE ALONE?

THE MOOR ALREADY CHANGES WITH MY POISONS...

...YOUR LADY...
...VEHE...
...MU...

WHICH AT THE FIRST ARE SCARCE FOUND TO DISTASTE, BUT WITH A LITTLE ART, BURN LIKE THE MINES OF SULPHUR.

I DID SAY SO... LOOK WHERE HE COMES!

NOT POPPY NOR ALL THE DROWSY SYRUPS OF THE WORLD SHALL EVER MEDICINE THEE TO SWEET SLEEP!

THOU HAST SET ME ON THE RACK!

O, NOW, FOR EVER FAREWELL THE TRANQUIL MIND! FAREWELL ALL PRIDE, POMP AND CIRCUMSTANCE OF GLORIOUS WAR! OTHELLO'S OCCUPATION'S GONE!

O MONSTROUS WORLD! TO BE DIRECT AND HONEST IS NOT SAFE.

VILLAIN, BE SURE THOU PROVE MY LOVE A WHORE, OR WOE UPON THY LIFE!

I'LL NOT ENDURE IT. WOULD I WERE SATISFIED!

HOW SATISFIED, MY LORD?

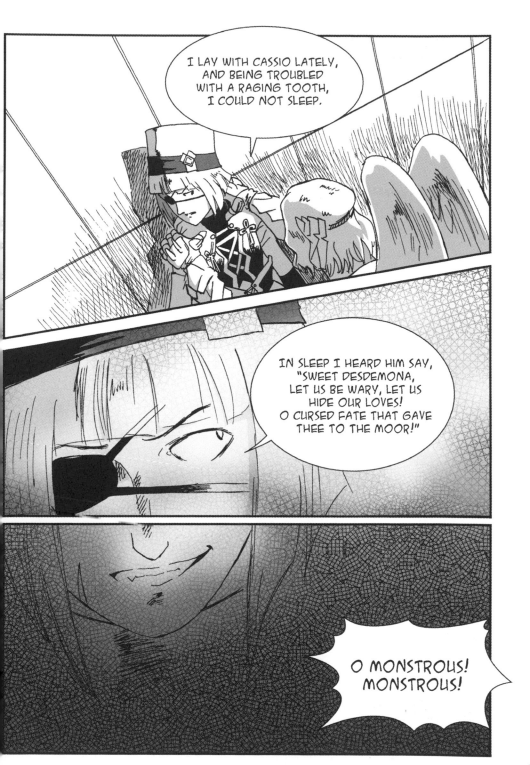

TELL ME THIS.

HAVE YOU NOT SEEN A HANDKERCHIEF IN YOUR WIFE'S HAND?

IT WAS MY FIRST GIFT.

IF IT BE THAT — ARISE, BLACK VENGEANCE, FROM HOLLOW HELL!

SUCH A HANDKERCHIEF DID I TODAY SEE CASSIO WIPE HIS BEARD WITH.

PATIENCE, I SAY, YOUR MIND PERHAPS MAY CHANGE.

NEVER, IAGO!

MY BLOODY THOUGHTS SHALL NEVER LOOK BACK TILL A WIDE REVENGE SWALLOW THEM UP.

WITNESS THAT HERE IAGO DOTH GIVE UP HIS WIT, HANDS, HEART TO WRONGED OTHELLO'S SERVICE!

LET HIM COMMAND.

WITHIN THESE THREE DAYS LET ME HEAR THEE SAY THAT CASSIO'S NOT ALIVE.

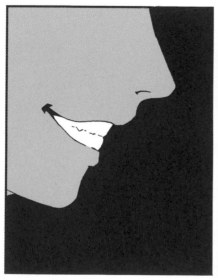

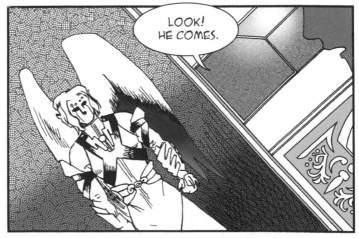

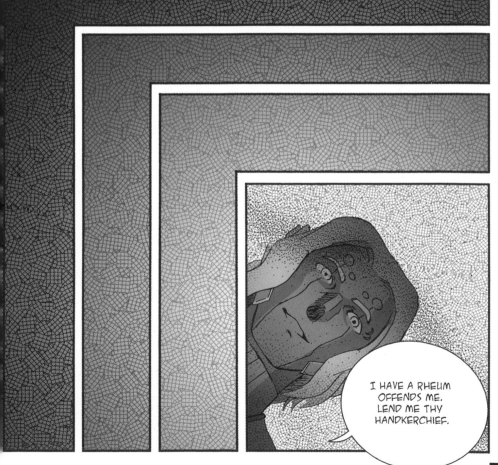

HERE, MY LORD.

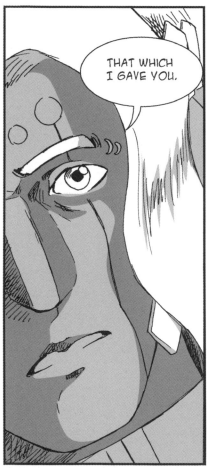

THAT WHICH I GAVE YOU.

I HAVE IT NOT ABOUT ME.

NOT? THAT'S A FAULT.

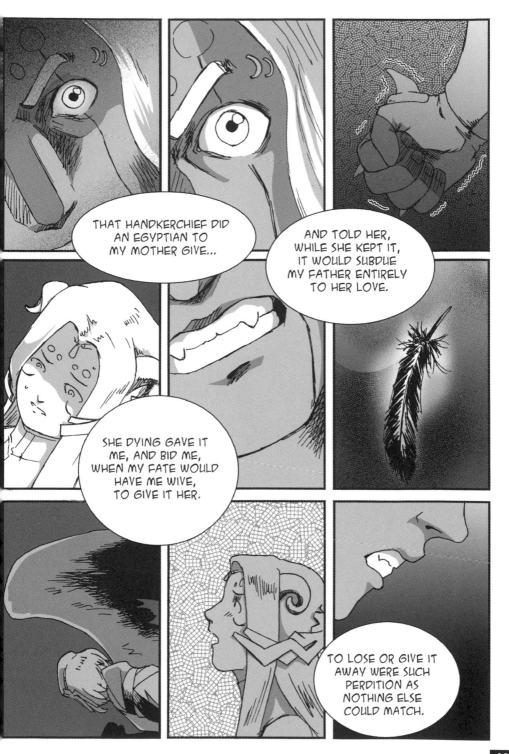

THAT HANDKERCHIEF DID AN EGYPTIAN TO MY MOTHER GIVE...

AND TOLD HER, WHILE SHE KEPT IT, IT WOULD SUBDUE MY FATHER ENTIRELY TO HER LOVE.

SHE DYING GAVE IT ME, AND BID ME, WHEN MY FATE WOULD HAVE ME WIVE, TO GIVE IT HER.

TO LOSE OR GIVE IT AWAY WERE SUCH PERDITION AS NOTHING ELSE COULD MATCH.

129

IS NOT THIS MAN JEALOUS?

I NEVER SAW THIS BEFORE.

SURE, THERE'S SOME WONDER IN THIS HANDKERCHIEF. I AM MOST UNHAPPY IN THE LOSS OF IT.

LOOK YOU – CASSIO AND MY HUSBAND.

134

SWEET BIANCA...

WHENCE CAME THIS? THIS IS SOME TOKEN FROM A NEWER FRIEND.

YOU ARE JEALOUS NOW THAT THIS IS FROM SOME MISTRESS? NO, BIANCA.

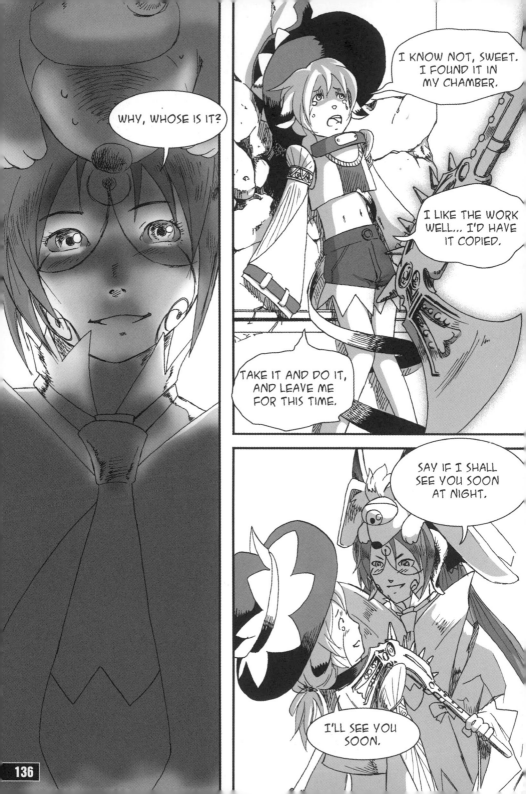

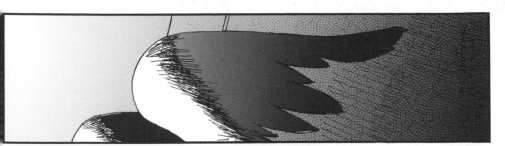

THOU SAID'ST HE HAD MY HANDKERCHIEF.

AY, WHAT OF THAT?

THAT'S NOT SO GOOD NOW. WHAT HATH HE SAID?

FAITH, THAT HE DID —

WHAT?

LIE –
WITH HER?!
WITH HER, ON HER, WHAT YOU WILL.
LIE WITH HER! LIE ON HER!
IT IS NOT WORDS THAT SHAKE ME THUS.
EARS AND LIPS!
IS IT POSSIBLE? CONFESS! HANDKERCHIEF! O DEVIL!

WHAT'S THE MATTER?

MY LORD IS FALLEN INTO AN EPILEPSY.

THIS IS HIS SECOND FIT. HE HAD ONE YESTERDAY.

LOOK! HE STIRS.

WITHDRAW YOURSELF A WHILE — I WOULD SPEAK WITH YOU.

HOW IS IT, GENERAL? HAVE YOU HURT YOUR HEAD?

DOST THOU MOCK ME?

NO, BY HEAVEN! BEAR YOUR FORTUNE LIKE A MAN!

DID HE CONFESS IT?

CASSIO CAME HITHER. I BID HIM RETURN AND HERE SPEAK WITH ME.

NOW IF THIS SUIT LAY IN BIANCA'S POWER, HOW QUICKLY SHOULD YOU SPEED!

I THINK, I'FAITH, SHE LOVES ME.

SHE GIVES IT OUT THAT YOU SHALL MARRY HER.

I MARRY HER! HA, HA, HA!

SO, SO, SO.
THEY LAUGH
THAT WIN.

IAGO BECKONS ME.
NOW HE BEGINS
THE STORY.

SHE HAUNTS ME
IN EVERY PLACE.

SHE FALLS ABOUT
MY NECK, HANGS
AND LOLLS AND
WEEPS UPON ME.
HA, HA, HA!

NOW HE TELLS
HOW SHE PLUCKED
HIM TO MY CHAMBER.

IF YOU'LL COME TO SUPPER TONIGHT, YOU MAY.

AFTER HER, AFTER HER.

I MUST — SHE'LL RAIL IN THE STREET ELSE.

GO TO, SAY NO MORE!

DID YOU PERCEIVE HOW HE LAUGHED?

AND DID YOU SEE THE HANDKERCHIEF?

WAS THAT MINE?

SEE HOW HE PRIZES THE FOOLISH WOMAN YOUR WIFE! SHE GAVE IT HIM AND HE HATH GIVEN IT HIS WHORE. NAY, YOU MUST FORGET THAT.

LET HER ROT AND PERISH AND BE DAMNED TONIGHT, FOR SHE SHALL NOT LIVE!

MY HEART IS TURNED TO STONE! I STRIKE IT AND IT HURTS MY HAND!

O, THE WORLD HATH NOT A SWEETER CREATURE!

SHE'S THE WORSE FOR ALL THIS.

BUT YET THE PITY OF IT, IAGO, THE PITY OF IT!

WHAT TRUMPET IS THAT?

'TIS LODOVICO, COME FROM VENICE, AND SEE, YOUR WIFE IS WITH HIM.

THE DUKE AND SENATORS OF VENICE GREET YOU.

FIRE AND BRIMSTONE!

WHAT! IS HE ANGRY?

MAYBE THE LETTER MOVED HIM. FOR, AS I THINK, THEY DO COMMAND HIM HOME, DEPUTING CASSIO IN HIS GOVERNMENT.

I AM GLAD ON IT.

MY LORD, THIS WOULD NOT BE BELIEVED IN VENICE.

MAKE HER AMENDS, SHE WEEPS.

IF THE EARTH COULD TEEM WITH WOMAN'S TEARS, EACH DROP WOULD PROVE A CROCODILE.

OUT OF MY SIGHT!

TRULY, AN OBEDIENT LADY. I DO BESEECH YOUR LORDSHIP, CALL HER BACK.

SHE CAN WEEP, SIR, AND SHE'S OBEDIENT, AS YOU SAY...

O WELL-PAINTED PASSION!

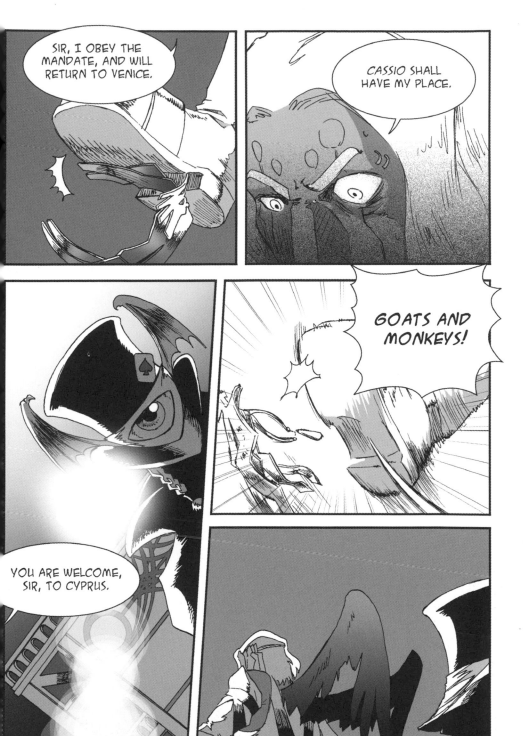

IS IT HIS USE? OR DID THE LETTERS WORK UPON HIS BLOOD?

ALAS, ALAS! IT IS NOT HONESTY IN ME TO SPEAK WHAT I HAVE SEEN AND KNOWN.

YOU SHALL OBSERVE HIM AND MARK HOW HE CONTINUES.

I AM SORRY THAT I AM DECEIVED IN HIM.

FOR, IF SHE BE NOT HONEST, CHASTE AND TRUE, THE PUREST OF HER SEX IS FOUL AS SLANDER.

BID HER COME HITHER.

IF ANY WRETCH HAVE PUT THIS IN YOUR HEAD, LET HEAVEN REQUITE IT WITH THE SERPENT'S CURSE!

THIS IS A SUBTLE WHORE, A LOCK AND KEY OF VILLAINOUS SECRETS...

WHAT'S THE MATTER, LADY?

HE CALLED HER "WHORE".

HAS SHE FORSOOK HER FATHER AND HER COUNTRY AND HER FRIENDS, TO BE CALLED WHORE?

HOW COMES THIS TRICK UPON HIM?

OME ETERNAL VILLAIN, O GET SOME OFFICE, EVISED THIS SLANDER.

THERE IS NO SUCH MAN.

O GOOD IAGO, WHAT SHALL I DO TO WIN MY LORD AGAIN?

FOR, BY THIS LIGHT OF HEAVEN, I KNOW NOT HOW I LOST HIM.

THE BUSINESS OF THE STATE DOES HIM OFFENCE...

GO IN, AND WEEP NOT. ALL THINGS SHALL BE WELL.

HOW NOW, RODERIGO?

I DO NOT FIND THAT THOU DEAL'ST JUSTLY WITH ME.

I HAVE WASTED MYSELF OUT OF MY MEANS.

THE JEWELS YOU HAD FROM ME TO DELIVER TO DESDEMONA, YOU TOLD ME SHE HAS RECEIVED, AND RETURNED ME EXPECTATIONS, BUT I FIND NONE.

CASSIO SUPS TONIGHT WITH A HARLOT.

IF YOU WILL WATCH HIS GOING THENCE, YOU MAY TAKE HIM AT YOUR PLEASURE.

I WILL BE NEAR TO SECOND YOUR ATTEMPT AND HE SHALL FALL BETWEEN US.

COME, STAND NOT AMAZED, BUT GO ALONG WITH ME.

HOW GOES IT NOW?

HE HATH COMMANDED ME TO GO TO BED AND BADE ME TO DISMISS YOU.

I WOULD YOU HAD NEVER SEEN HIM.

SO WOULD NOT I. MY LOVE DOTH SO APPROVE HIM THAT EVEN HIS FROWNS HAVE GRACE.

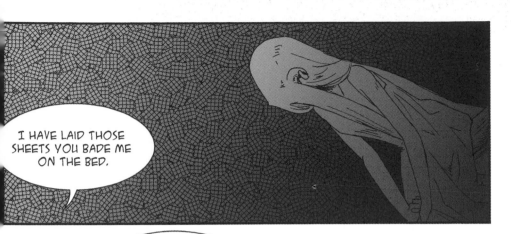

I HAVE LAID THOSE SHEETS YOU BADE ME ON THE BED.

IF I DO DIE BEFORE THEE, PRITHEE SHROUD ME IN ONE OF THOSE SAME SHEETS.

COME, COME, YOU TALK.

MY MOTHER HAD A MAID CALLED BARBARA. SHE WAS IN LOVE, AND HE SHE LOVED DID FORSAKE HER.

Spin

Spin

SHE HAD A SONG OF "WILLOW", AND SHE DIED SINGING IT.

THAT SONG TONIGHT WILL NOT GO FROM MY MIND...

The fresh streams ran by her
and murmured her moans,

Sing willow, willow, willow.

Her salt tears fell from her
and softened the stones—

Sing willow, willow, willow...

Sing all a green willow must be my garland.
Let nobody blame him, his scorn I approve

MINE EYES DO ITCH. DOTH THAT BODE WEEPING?

O, THESE MEN, THESE MEN!

LET THEM USE US WELL: ELSE LET THEM KNOW, THE ILLS WE DO, THEIR ILLS INSTRUCT US SO.

HEAVEN ME SUCH USAGE SEND!

GOOD NIGHT, GOOD NIGHT.

WEAR THY RAPIER BARE.

QUICK, QUICK, FEAR NOTHING! I'LL BE AT THY ELBOW.

BE NEAR AT HAND. I HAVE NO GREAT DEVOTION TO THE DEED.

WHETHER HE KILL CASSIO OR CASSIO HIM, OR EACH DO KILL THE OTHER, EVERY WAY MAKES MY GAIN.

LIVE RODERIGO, HE CALLS ME TO A RESTITUTION OF GOLD AND JEWELS THAT I BOBBED FROM HIM AS GIFTS TO DESDEMONA...

IF CASSIO DO REMAIN, THE MOOR MAY UNFOLD ME TO HIM.

THERE STAND I IN MUCH PERIL. NO, HE MUST DIE.

'TIS HE. VILLAIN, THOU DIEST!

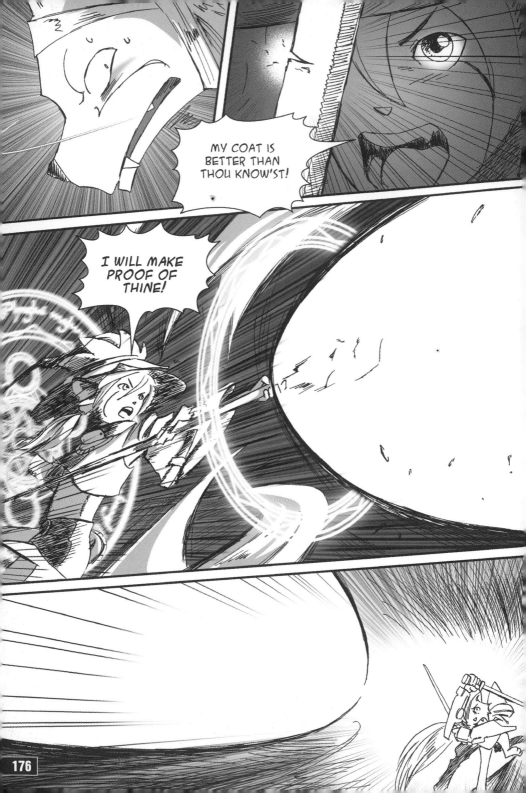

MY LEG IS CUT IN TWO.

LIGHT, GENTLEMEN. I'LL BIND IT WITH MY SHIRT.

CASSIO

O MY DEAR CASSIO!

KNOW WE THIS FACE OR NO?

ALAS, MY DEAR COUNTRYMAN, RODERIGO?

YES, SURE! O HEAVEN, RODERIGO!

WHAT, OF VENICE?

EMILIA, RUN TO THE CITADEL AND TELL MY LORD AND LADY WHAT HATH HAPP'D.

THIS IS THE NIGHT THAT EITHER MAKES ME OR FORDOES ME QUITE.

IT IS THE CAUSE, THE CAUSE, MY SOUL!

YET I'LL NOT SHED HER BLOOD, NOR SCAR THAT WHITER SKIN OF HERS THAN SNOW.

YET SHE MUST DIE, ELSE SHE'LL BETRAY MORE MEN.

PUT OUT THE LIGHT — AND THEN PUT OUT THE LIGHT!

I WILL KILL THEE, AND LOVE THEE AFTER.

THIS SORROW STRIKES WHERE IT DOTH LOVE.

SHE WAKES...

OTHELLO?

HAVE YOU PRAYED TONIGHT, DESDEMONA?

189

'TIS EMILIA,
SHE COMES TO SPEAK
OF CASSIO'S DEATH.

O HEAVY HOUR!
METHINKS IT SHOULD
BE NOW A HUGE
ECLIPSE OF SUN
AND MOON, AND THAT
THE AFFRIGHTED GLOBE
SHOULD YAWN
AT ALTERATION.

BAM!

BAM!

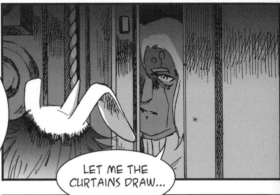

LET ME THE
CURTAINS DRAW...

CASSIO, MY LORD,
HAS KILLED A YOUNG
VENETIAN CALLED
RODERIGO!

A WICKED LIE! SHE FALSE WITH CASSIO?

I THINK I SMELL IT! O VILLAINY!

POOR DESDEMONA! I AM GLAD THY FATHER'S DEAD. THY MATCH WAS MORTAL TO HIM.

'TIS PITIFUL, BUT YET IAGO KNOWS.

CASSIO CONFESSED IT. I SAW IN HIS HAND A HANDKERCHIEF MY FATHER GAVE MY MOTHER.

O HEAVENLY POWERS!

HOLD YOUR PEACE.

O THOU DULL MOOR! THAT HANDKERCHIEF MY HUSBAND OFTEN BEGGED OF ME TO STEAL!

HE'S GONE.

TAKE THIS WEAPON I HAVE RECOVERED FROM THE MOOR. LET HIM NOT PASS.

I'LL AFTER THAT VILLAIN...

WHAT DID THY SONG BODE, LADY?

I WILL PLAY THE SWAN AND DIE IN MUSIC — "WILLOW, WILLOW, WILLOW..."

SHE WAS CHASTE. SHE LOVED THEE, CRUEL MOOR.

MOOR...

SO COME MY SOUL TO BLISS AS I SPEAK TRUE.

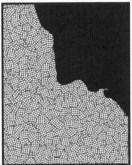

WHO CAN CONTROL HIS FATE? COLD, COLD, MY GIRL, EVEN LIKE THY CHASTITY.

WHIP ME, YE DEVILS!

BLOW ME ABOUT IN WINDS! ROAST ME IN SULPHUR! WASH ME IN STEEP-DOWN GULFS OF LIQUID FIRE!

O DESDEMONA! DEAD! DESDEMONA!

IF THAT THOU BE'ST A DEVIL, I CANNOT KILL THEE!

I BLEED, SIR, BUT NOT KILLED.

WILL YOU DEMAND THAT DEMI-DEVIL WHY HE HATH THUS ENSNARED MY SOUL AND BODY?

DEMAND ME NOTHING. WHAT YOU KNOW, YOU KNOW. FROM THIS TIME FORTH I NEVER WILL SPEAK WORD.

YOUR POWER AND YOUR COMMAND IS TAKEN OFF, AND CASSIO RULES IN CYPRUS.

FOR THIS SLAVE, IF THERE BE ANY CUNNING CRUELTY THAT CAN TORMENT HIM MUCH, IT SHALL BE HIS.

WHEN YOU SHALL THESE UNLUCKY DEEDS RELATE, SPEAK OF ME AS I AM, NOTHING EXTENUATE.

THEN MUST YOU SPEAK OF ONE THAT LOVED NOT WISELY, BUT TOO WELL.

I KISSED THEE ERE I KILLED THEE — NO WAY BUT THIS, KILLING MYSELF TO DIE UPON A KISS.

LOOK ON THE TRAGIC LOADING OF THIS BED. THIS IS THY WORK.

MYSELF WILL STRAIGHT ABOARD, AND TO THE STATE THIS HEAVY ACT WITH HEAVY HEART RELATE.

PLOT SUMMARY OF OTHELLO

The scene is Venice during Carnival time when masks, costumes and fantasies take over from normal life. Othello – a former slave, now commander-in-chief of the Venetian Army – has eloped with Desdemona, the daughter of local dignitary Brabantio. But Othello has made a dangerous enemy: by promoting the loyal Cassio to be his Lieutenant-General, he leaves his junior officer Iago deeply resentful at being passed over.

Iago plots his revenge, persuading Roderigo (an unsuccessful suitor to Desdemona) to inform Brabantio of Othello's marriage to his daughter. Meanwhile, the Duke of Venice requires Othello's services: the Turks are sailing for Cyprus. Othello sets sail at the head of a task force, with his wife and staff. By the time they arrive, though, the Turkish fleet has shipwrecked.

Seizing the opportunity, Iago contrives to dupe Othello into thinking that Cassio is having an affair with Desdemona. He plies Cassio with drink, persuades Roderigo to pick a quarrel with him, and looks on as Cassio attacks the Governor of Cyprus, Montano. Cassio is disgraced, and Othello discharges him from his command. At Iago's suggestion, Cassio approaches Desdemona to persuade Othello to forgive him. Desdemona agrees, but Iago ensures that her pleas will be misconstrued, by insinuating to Othello that she and Cassio are lovers.

Othello, maddened by jealousy, needs proof of the adultery. This Iago supplies in the form of the handkerchief Desdemona accidentally drops and which Emilia, Iago's wife, retrieves. Iago leaves the handkerchief in Cassio's rooms – and Cassio in turn gives it to his girlfriend Bianca. Iago now stages a meeting with Cassio, knowing that Othello will overhear and misinterpret their words about Bianca as references to Desdemona. Then Bianca arrives, complaining to Cassio that the handkerchief he gave her was from another woman. Apparently confirmed in his worst suspicions, Othello vows to murder Desdemona, and Iago promises to murder Cassio.

Meanwhile Lodovico brings news that Othello has been recalled to Venice, and relieved of his command by Cassio. Enraged, and suspecting the worst, Othello publicly strikes Desdemona. Iago seeks to tie up his plot by inciting Roderigo to kill Cassio. But the ambush goes wrong and, after covertly wounding Cassio from behind, Iago kills Roderigo to shut him up. Iago's intrigues are unravelling – but not before Othello has strangled Desdemona in her bed.

Emilia arrives with news of Roderigo's death, but cries out for help when she sees Desdemona dying. Montano, Gratiano and Iago arrive and Emilia explains how the handkerchief was lost. Iago kills Emilia and flees, but is captured; having discovered his plot, Othello wounds Iago, then kills himself.

A BRIEF LIFE OF WILLIAM SHAKESPEARE

Shakespeare's birthday is traditionally said to be the 23rd of April — St George's Day, patron saint of England. A good start for England's greatest writer. But that date and even his name are uncertain. He signed his own name in different ways. "Shakespeare" is now the accepted one out of dozens of different versions.

He was born at Stratford-upon-Avon in 1564, and baptized on 26th April. His mother, Mary Arden, was the daughter of a prosperous farmer. His father, John Shakespeare, a glove-maker, was a respected civic figure — and probably also a Catholic. In 1570, just as Will began school, his father was accused of illegal dealings. The family fell into debt and disrepute.

Will attended a local school for eight years. He did not go to university. The next ten years are a blank filled by suppositions. Was he briefly a Latin teacher, a soldier, a sea-faring explorer? Was he prosecuted and whipped for poaching deer?

We do know that in 1582 he married Anne Hathaway, eight years his senior, and three months pregnant. Two more children — twins — were born three years later but, by around 1590, Will had left Stratford to pursue a theatre career in London. Shakespeare's apprenticeship began as an actor and "pen for hire".

He learned his craft the hard way. He soon won fame as a playwright with often-staged popular hits.

He and his colleagues formed a stage company, the Lord Chamberlain's Men, which built the famous Globe Theatre. It opened in 1599 but was destroyed by fire in 1613 during a performance of *Henry VIII* which used gunpowder special effects. It was rebuilt in brick the following year.

Shakespeare was a financially successful writer who invested his money wisely in property. In 1597, he bought an enormous house in Stratford, and in 1608 became a shareholder in London's Blackfriars Theatre. He also redeemed the family's honour by acquiring a personal coat of arms.

Shakespeare wrote over 40 works, including poems, "lost" plays and collaborations, in a career spanning nearly 25 years. He retired to Stratford in 1613, where he died on 23rd April 1616, aged 52, apparently of a fever after a "merry meeting" of drinks with friends. Shakespeare did in fact die on St George's Day! He was buried "full 17 foot deep" in Holy Trinity Church, Stratford, and left an epitaph cursing anyone who dared disturb his bones.

There have been preposterous theories disputing Shakespeare's authorship. Some claim that Sir Francis Bacon (1561–1626), philosopher and Lord Chancellor, was the real author of Shakespeare's plays. Others propose Edward de Vere, Earl of Oxford (1550–1604), or, even more weirdly, Queen Elizabeth I. The implication is that the "real" Shakespeare had to be a university graduate or an aristocrat. Nothing less would do for the world's greatest writer.

Shakespeare is mysteriously hidden behind his work. His life will not tell us what inspired his genius.

MANGA SHAKESPEARE ®

EDITORIAL

Richard Appignanesi: Text Adaptor

Richard Appignanesi was a founder and co-director of the Writers & Readers Publishing Cooperative and Icon Books where he originated the internationally acclaimed *Introducing* series. His own best-selling titles in the series include *Freud*, *Postmodernism* and *Existentialism*. He is also the author of the fiction trilogy *Italia Perversa* and the novel *Yukio Mishima's Report to the Emperor*. Currently associate editor of the journal *Third Text* and reviews editor of the journal *Futures*, his latest book *What do Existentialists Believe?* was released in 2006.

Nick de Somogyi: Textual Consultant

Nick de Somogyi works as a freelance writer and researcher, as a genealogist at the College of Arms, and as a contributing editor to *New Theatre Quarterly*. He is the founding editor of the *Globe Quartos* series, and was the visiting curator at Shakespeare's Globe, 2003–6. His publications include *Shakespeare's Theatre of War* (1998), *Jokermen and Thieves: Bob Dylan and the Ballad Tradition* (1986), and (from 2001) the *Shakespeare Folios* series for Nick Hern Books. He has also contributed to the Open University (1995), Carlton Television (2000), and BBC Radio 3 and Radio 4.

ARTIST

Ryuta Osada

Ryuta Osada is a Japanese-born manga artist, now living in London. Educated in Japan, Ryuta read History at Nihon University, writing his thesis on the Elizabethan era, and gained qualifications to teach History and Sociology. After moving to England in 1994 to study English, he took an Art Foundation diploma in 1999, followed by a degree in Graphic Design at The Surrey Institute of Art and Design (2002–2005). In 2006 he joined the prestigious Central Saint Martins Graphic Design and Illustration course. He is presently collaborating on a guide to drawing manga.

PUBLISHER

SelfMadeHero is a UK-based manga and graphic novel imprint, reinventing some of the most important works of European and world literature. In 2008 SelfMadeHero was named **UK Young Publisher of the Year** at the prestigious British Book Industry Awards.

OTHER TITLES IN THIS SERIES INCLUDE

Much Ado About Nothing, *King Lear*, *Henry VIII*, *Twelfth Night*, *The Merchant of Venice* and *The Taming of the Shrew*.

SELF MADE HERO

www.selfmadehero.com